MW01518532

THIS HOTEL

THIS HOTEL

Alex Poch-Goldin

This Hotel
first published 2002 by
Scirocco Drama
An imprint of J. Gordon Shillingford Publishing Inc.
© 2001 Alex Poch-Goldin

Scirocco Drama Editor: Glenda MacFarlane
Cover design by Terry Gallagher/Doowah Design Inc.
Cover photograph by David Kinsman
Author photo by Kelly Thornton
Printed and bound in Canada

We acknowledge the financial support of The Canada Council for the Arts
and the Manitoba Arts Council for our publishing program.

All rights reserved. No part of this book may be reproduced, for any reason, by any means, without the permission of the publisher. This play is fully protected under the copyright laws of Canada and all other countries of the Copyright Union and is subject to royalty. Changes to the text are expressly forbidden without written consent of the author. Rights to produce, film, record in whole or in part, in any medium or in any language, by any group amateur or professional, are retained by the author.
Production inquiries should be addressed to:
Rich Caplan, The Noble Caplan Agency
1260 Yonge Street, 2nd Floor
Toronto, Ontario M4T 1W6
Phone: (416) 920-5385
Fax: (416) 920-6343

Canadian Cataloguing in Publication Data

Poch-Goldin, Alex
    This hotel
A play.
ISBN 1-896239-87-0
    I. Title.
PS8581.O15T48 2002   C812'.54   C2002-900245-1
PR9199.4.P628T48 2002

J. Gordon Shillingford Publishing
P.O. Box 86, 905 Corydon Avenue, Winnipeg, MB Canada R3M 3S3

For Kelly—who believes in me beyond my understanding.

Acknowledgements

I am indebted to:

The ghosts that haunt this story.

Layne Coleman, Jacoba Knappen, Martha Ferguson, The Canada Council for the Arts, Laidlaw Foundation, Ontario Arts Council and Toronto Arts Council, CanStage, Marty Bragg, Janese Kane, Glenda MacFarlane and Gordon Shillingford, my incredible family, the Passe Muraille production staff, Taylor Raths, David Kinsman, Jon Kaplan, Kevin Connolly, Steve Lucas, Millennium Partnership Foundation, Toronto Fringe, the box office girls, Iris Turcott, the cast who gave it blood, and Kelly, who shaped the story.

Alex Poch-Goldin

Alex Poch-Goldin is an actor and writer from Montreal. He trained in acting at The Dome Theatre and later studied at the National Theater Institute in Connecticut. His plays include *Jim and Shorty*, *The Gospel According to Jude*, *Cringeworthy* and *Anybody and Nobody*. His work has been produced at Theatre Passe Muraille, Buddies in Bad Times, Factory Theatre and Canadian Stage, for whom he is currently developing a new project. He continues to work on his novel *Racing Car Pajamas*. He lives in Toronto.

Production History

This Hotel received its mainstage premiere in May, 2001, as a Planet 88 production (in association with Theatre Passe Muraille) at Theatre Passe Muraille, Toronto, with the following cast:

ARLENE, ESTELLE .... Brenda Bazinet
LESTER .... Randy Hughson
LOUISE/ANTOINETTE .... Veronika Hurnik
BELLHOP .... Alon Nashman
PETER/REX/MONTY .... Richard Zeppieri

Directed by Kelly Thornton
Set Design by Steve Lucas
Lighting Design by Peter Freund
Costume Design by Angela Thomas
Compositions/Sound Design by Richard Feren
Choreography by Gizella Witkowsky
Stage Manager: J.P. Robichaud
Assistant Stage Management: Zoe Carpenter and Trina Sookhai

This Hotel was first produced in the 1998 Fringe of Toronto Festival with: Randy Hughson, Veronika Hurnik, Alon Nashman, Giselle Rousseau and Richard Zeppieri. Directed by Kelly Thornton; Set and Costume Design by Kelly Wolf; Music by Brian Cram, Choreography by Gizella Witkowsky; Lighting by Peter Freund; Stage Management by Laura Rubino; Co-produced with New Globe Theatre, Janese Kane and Martha Ferguson.

Characters

	LESTER, a man on the edge
	ARLENE, Lester's wife
	PETER, Arlene's lover
The Guests	ESTELLE, a faded beauty
	REX, a Latino playboy
	MONTY, a closeted homosexual
	LOUISE, a sexy loner
	The FIGURE
The Staff	ANTOINETTE, the French chambermaid
	The BELLHOP (This character is a shape shifter.
	His roles in the hotel include the waiter, the
	handyman, the manager, the bartender, the
	lounge singer and the hustler.)

The following roles are to be doubled: Arlene and Estelle; Antoinette and Louise; Rex, Peter, Monty and the Figure. The Bellhop and various. The cast is made up of five actors.

Set

The set consists of five doors converging on a bed centre stage. All action takes place in the same room with various alterations to the space. Locations: Lester and Arlene's house, the hotel (Lester's mind), the front desk, Lester's room, Estelle's room, Louise's room, the Restaurant, and the Bar Lounge.

Playwright's Note

This Hotel is a fantastical play. The story takes place in the protagonist's mind and therefore anything is possible. There are flashbacks, fantasies, and even a dance number. The play is highly physical and although it is not a farce, it requires the same crisp timing. Some scenes are quite filmic and this approach is not wrong. Actors play multiple roles and yet should be separate characters.

The transformation from Lester's house to the hotel should be highly theatrical and ultimately take the audience's breath away.

The first production of this play employed a magic bed that was manipulated by the Bellhop and transformed from the sofa to the hotel bed to the dining room table, the front desk and the bar. Curtains from the house opened and the doors of the hotel closed in their place. Theatricality is the key here, constantly jarring the audience with magical transformations and surprising appearances.

The Bellhop is a shape shifter, the host who opens and closes the play and in-between becomes the male staff of the hotel. While each character he plays is distinct, he is not trying to fool the audience into thinking he is a different person each time.

Antoinette the chambermaid is an ethereal presence in the play. She holds some elusive secret. Sometimes she is present and not seen; other times she may be spoken to.

Scene 1

Lester's House

> *ARLENE is in the living room with PETER, they are holding drinks. She is wearing a fashionable outfit with jewelry. He wears a leather jacket and jeans.*

ARLENE: It wasn't the price that upset me, but it didn't come in any other colour. I want a blue one. I'm buying the sofa. I won't pay for something I don't want. *(Beat.)* Things have to match. This room has no... It has to be completely redone.

> *She smiles. PETER smiles back. There is a sexual tension. She moves closer.*

I like the lines on your mouth. They make me hungry.

PETER: You smell nice.

ARLENE: Sandalwood.

> *We hear the sound of keys. The door opens and LESTER enters in a hat and trench coat with a briefcase and a bouquet of flowers.*

LESTER: Sorry I'm late I got... *(Pause as he sees them.)* What's going on?

> *Silence. LESTER cautiously crosses to ARLENE.*

Who's this?

ARLENE: You're early. *(She turns to PETER.)*

Silence.

LESTER: I brought you some flowers…

ARLENE: Stick them in a book.

            Silence.

LESTER: Arlene… *(Pause.)* I know, I'll make us all a drink, we can relax and…

            ARLENE and PETER both drink from the drinks they have. ARLENE remains fixed on PETER.

LESTER: Well okay. I guess I'll…I'll just go.

            He walks to the door with the flowers, opens the door and starts to leave.

            Okay I'm going.

ARLENE: Bye.

            LESTER laughs and re-enters. He crosses to ARLENE and speaks desperate and low.

LESTER: Arlene don't do this. Please. We don't have to do this.

            ARLENE crosses to PETER and gives him a sensual kiss. She turns to LESTER.

ARLENE: Fix yourself a drink.

            ARLENE pulls PETER out of the room. LESTER stands staring after the two of them. He steps towards them and stops, not knowing if he should stay or go. He picks up his briefcase and still holds the flowers. Finally he sits on the couch in shock. Time stops. Sound builds. The BELLHOP emerges from behind the couch, spawned from LESTER's mind. An eerie presence. A fly buzzes.

BELLHOP: And the fly buzzes and flaps its tiny wings. Climbs the walls seeking sustenance. Its existence is all it knows.

> *LESTER stands and walks to the front door. He opens it. In unison the living room curtains disappear and five doors close in their place as the house dramatically transforms into the hotel. The walls change colour. LESTER exits. A "Vacancy" sign appears.*

Scene 2

The Hotel

BELLHOP: And in its search it finds itself on the sticky steps of a spider's house. And with all its strength tries to free itself, only sticking more against strands of silk, inlaid with bits of fruit and wings of yesterday's supper. And it watches as the master of the manor on eight giant limbs approaches to dissect the unexpected dinner guest into appetizers and dessert. And the fly buzzes, its tiny wings trapped. Immobile. Panicked. It yearns, for the promise of release.

> *A door opens and LESTER stands there in silhouette.*

This hotel was designed with you in mind. The doors are doors to secrets. Broken dreams and empty halls. *(Addressing LESTER.)* Been here as long as anyone can remember. *(He offers him a book.)* Sign the register. Whatever name you like. Spend the night. Mr. Lester. Queen size beds, walk-in closets, and room service never stops. I'll help store your baggage. A valise of betrayal or jealousy. A satchel of ecstasy or a chest of desire. I'm at your service. At your convenience. Twenty four hours a day. *(The BELLHOP holds up a key.)* Room 3. *(The BELLHOP exits.)*

Randy Hughson as Lester, Alon Nashman as the Bellhop.

Scene 3

> *LESTER takes the key and locks the door. He puts down his briefcase and looks around confused as to where he is. LESTER is in bad shape. He rubs his face. Clearly uncomfortable with things. He sits on the bed. We hear creaking from the floor above. LESTER stands up. He walks around. He sits on a chair and looks at the bouquet of flowers. He drops the flowers on the floor. We hear footsteps walking above him. He opens the closet and from his coat he pulls out a vial of pills and takes two. He rubs his face in his hands and notices a radio on the shelf. He turns it on and hears:*

ARLENE: "Oh, oh, oh, oh, oh, oh, oh, ya."

> *He flips the station and hears:*

Fix yourself a drink.

> *He flips the station and hears:*

Do it! Do it! Do me!

> *He turns off the radio and puts it in the closet.*

Scene 3A

> *We hear a mournful French song. He sits on the bed.*

ANTOINETTE: Toutes les nuits sont faites a d'eau
Les jours s'ecoulent goutte a goutte
Ton depart, mon amour m'a laisse
Assoiffe.
Mais j'irai puise une source
Qui s'alimente de l'interieur
Et plus jamais, de mes yeux,
Les l'armes ne s'echapperont.

(All the nights are water
One day drips into the next
And you, my love have left me
Drained and dry
But I will sprout a fountain
That will water from within
And tears won't ever
Tumble from my eye)

> ANTOINETTE *the chambermaid, still singing, comes into his room with two pillows. As* LESTER *moves to lie down she places a pillow under his head. He does not notice her as he drifts off. She picks up a flower from the bouquet, and smells it. She leaves with the flower, humming softly.* LESTER *wakes up at the last moment but she is gone. He goes to the door and opens it.*

LESTER: Is someone there?

Scene 4

> *We hear a buzzing fly enter the room.* PETER *and* ARLENE *arrive simultaneously, kissing passionately, getting on the bed.* LESTER *watches them.*

PETER: Was that your husband?

ARLENE: Yes.

> *They continue kissing.*

PETER: So how does that work?

ARLENE: I wanted more. He gave me less. So I learned to improvise.

> *They continue kissing.*

PETER: So it's a thing you do, he lets you do this?

ARLENE: What do you care?

PETER: *(Stopping her.)* I'm doing a study. I just wanna know.

ARLENE: Listen, don't talk. Talking ruins things.

           She kisses him.

PETER: So is this a game?

ARLENE: Yah.

PETER: Is he impotent or what?

ARLENE: Touch my neck.

PETER: I want to know what I'm scratching. He just won't do it or what?

ARLENE: All right forget it. I didn't bring you here for this.

PETER: I'm just asking.

ARLENE: You should go.

PETER: Is that what you want?

ARLENE: I want you to shut up!

           PETER gets up to leave.

           I'm sorry. I'm sorry. I didn't mean it. Forgive me please.

           Pause.

PETER: Is he still here?

ARLENE: Yup.

PETER: Come here.

           She approaches. He pulls off his shirt.

           Touch this. *(She touches his nipple. He kisses her. They start to get it on as LESTER watches. Eventually they disappear.)*

Scene 5

> *The BELLHOP, dressed as a waiter, appears and escorts LESTER into the dining room.*

BELLHOP: You're certain to find something to tempt you. A taste sure to linger.

> *He seats him in a chair stage right. Lights come up on LOUISE, sitting alone stage left with a napkin around her neck.*

The Widow's Lounge is revered for its table d'hôte.

> *He ties a napkin around LESTER's neck and hands him the menu.*

Peruse at your pleasure. Selections are designed to satisfy the most discerning connoisseur. As we say, if there's a hunger in your belly, and your loins have turned to jelly, then you're welcome to our venue. Choose an item from our menu.

> *LESTER notices LOUISE; he is struck by her beauty. The BELLHOP spreads a tablecloth on the bed between them. Music begins. The BELLHOP crosses to LOUISE, and they perform a torrid tango as he describes the following sexual delicacies:*

Appetizers tonight include: innocent kisses of childhood; the nibble, and the peck. Or you may prefer the angst of the teens consisting of soft touches on a bed of greens, or French kisses in a pool of white sauce. Elegant seconds follow with a spicy gamahuche accompanied by over-stuffed Viennese oysters. For an entree you may enjoy a scrumptious cuissade or an aromatic flanquette. Both a la carte. And I recommend the decadent la negresse if you've a taste for something exotic. If still tempted, try the creamy pompoir, ligottage a la mode, and finishing up with a to-die-for, petite mort.

The Tango. Veronika Hurnik and Alon Nashman.

LOUISE, now sprawled on LESTER's lap, sighs with ecstasy. She then whirls back to her chair and wipes the sides of her mouth with her napkin and sits as if nothing has happened except in LESTER's mind. The BELLHOP crosses to LESTER.

BELLHOP: May I take your order?

LESTER: I need some time.

The BELLHOP leaves. Silence.

Scene 5A

LESTER: *(Hesitant.)* Hello.

Silence.

Have you eaten?

LOUISE: No.

Silence.

LESTER: Have you been here a long time?

LOUISE: Yes.

Silence.

LESTER: I've only just arrived. *(Pause.)* I don't plan a long stay.

LOUISE: Un huh.

LESTER: I sometimes walked by this hotel but I never came in.

LOUISE: It comes to you. It swallows you whole.

LESTER: I got lost in the hallways.

LOUISE: You'll get used to it.

Pause.

LESTER: There's a smell in this place a musty, sour... Do you smell it?

LOUISE: I have no sense of smell.

They stare at each other.

LESTER: You'll think I'm stupid for saying this but you're—

LOUISE/
LESTER: Very beautiful.

Silence.

LESTER: I'm so stupid.

LOUISE: I have a scar that stretches over my shoulder down my left breast to my rib cage. My nipple is a leather stub. *(Pause.)* Concentrate on that. *(Pause.)* It'll distract you.

LESTER: How did it happen?

She undoes her napkin, crosses to LESTER, and stares into his eyes.

LOUISE: Someone told me I was beautiful. And I believed him. *(She touches his face and drops the napkin in his lap.)*

LESTER: What do you want?

She begins to go, stops and turns.

LOUISE: *(Nonchalantly.)* Power. *(She exits.)*

LESTER smells the perfume on her napkin. The BELLHOP returns.

BELLHOP: Shall I bring it to your room?

Silence. LESTER sits for a bit. Then leaves.

Scene 6

> *Sound of laughter. ESTELLE enters her room with REX, leaving the door ajar. ESTELLE is dressed like a Tennessee Williams heroine. She sounds from Louisiana. REX wears a black velvet jacket and a white shirt; he speaks with a Mediterranean accent.*

REX: I said I'd see you to your room. There, a gentleman's promise. Now perhaps we might share a night cap.

ESTELLE: I can't invite you in.

REX: But why?

ESTELLE: I don't even know your name.

REX: I told you. My name is Rex.

ESTELLE: Rex is the Latin for king.

REX: Yes it is.

ESTELLE: It's also a dog's name. Goodnight.

REX: I won't bite. A gentleman's promise.

ESTELLE: Well perhaps for a minute. But only one. My lover's away on a trip and I expect him at any moment.

> *LESTER appears unseen in the doorway looking in. He watches the scene.*

REX: What smell are you wearing?

ESTELLE: Juniper. Do you have a gift for me?

REX: A gift?

ESTELLE: A true gentleman always presents a gift. I have green glass bottles from Trinidad. Yellow spices from Spain. Trinkets and gewgaws from around the globe.

REX: What do you do with them?

ESTELLE: Keep them, silly. In my closet. They're mementos. To remember.

REX: I'd love to take a peek.

ESTELLE: No. You can't see them. They're private. My private things. No. You shouldn't be so nosy.

REX: I have a curious nature.

ESTELLE: I have a collection of dried flowers too, pressed in my favourite books.

REX: Perhaps I could leaf through and smell them.

ESTELLE: This is only our first acquaintance.

                Beat.

REX: Where did he go?

ESTELLE: Who?

REX: Your lover.

ESTELLE: Oh. Constantinople. He's seeking an elusive mountain essence for me. To scent my baths.

REX: When exactly do you expect him?

ESTELLE: Oh. Well. It could be tonight. Perhaps tomorrow.

REX: So soon.

ESTELLE: Next week perhaps. But very soon. He's in Bombay haggling over some hand-spun silk. For me to fashion a gown.

REX: How wonderful. *(He takes her hand.)* You know, I've never met an Estelle before. Estelle. It's like a waterfall. It's like a magic spell. Time stops when I say it. Estelle.

ESTELLE: I am suddenly feeling so terribly tired. Please excuse me, Mr. Rex. I think I am unwell.

REX: Estelle, this hotel is a lonely place. The rooms are drafty and the halls are dim. And you. You're very beautiful. And lonely. Just like me.

ESTELLE: I must rise early in case he arrives. Now I really must retire.

REX: What is this. You joined me at my table.

ESTELLE: Thank you for your company. Now I must insist.

REX: I've treated you like a lady.

ESTELLE: And I am much obliged. Good night.

REX: You're wanting me to go?

ESTELLE: He's coming back.

REX: I bought you champagne!

ESTELLE: I'm waiting for my lover, Mr. Rex.

REX: What lover? The one in the sky buying you the moon?

ESTELLE: Doesn't fidelity mean anything to you?

REX: You're crazy.

ESTELLE: I'm waiting for the man I love! *(He leaves.)* I'm waiting for the man I love.

            The lights fade to black except for LESTER standing in the doorway.

Scene 7

            LESTER enters his room and turns on the light. A fly buzzes. He lays on the bed, hands over his eyes. He sits up and picks up the TV remote. We hear the following as he flips stations.

LESTER: I've been observing you.

ARLENE: Oh.

LESTER: From over there. You're very beautiful.

ARLENE: I see.

          Flip.

LESTER: From over there. You're very beautiful.

ARLENE: I see.

          Flip.

LESTER: I've been observing you.

ARLENE: Oh.

          Flip.

ARLENE: Oh, oh, oh ya, ya, ya, Oh!

MAN: You like that.

ARLENE: Mmmhm.

MAN: You like that.

          Tacky porn music plays. LESTER watches for a bit. The door opens and the BELLHOP comes in dressed as a handyman. LESTER is oblivious. The BELLHOP shakes his keys. LESTER turns.

Scene 8

LESTER: How did you get in?

BELLHOP: I have keys. They jangle when I walk.

LESTER: Are you here to fix something?

BELLHOP: Oh no.

LESTER: What do you want? I want to be alone.

BELLHOP: You are alone. But I can take you further.

LESTER: What?

BELLHOP: I have keys that open places you haven't been yet. How can you refuse an open door?

LESTER: I don't want to go anywhere.

The BELLHOP follows the flight of a wayward fly landing on the bed.

BELLHOP: You don't have to cross the threshold. *(He pulls out a fly swatter and whacks the fly.)* You can watch from afar. *(He puts the dead fly in his tool belt.)* That's what being alone is. Isolated in the company of others.

LESTER: Not now. I have some thinking to do.

BELLHOP: Thinking never did no good for no one. You have five beautiful senses, why deny them pleasure?

LESTER pushes him out of the room. The BELLHOP opens the door again.

I have keys that jangle.

The BELLHOP shakes his keys as LESTER locks the door.

Scene 8A

LESTER alone in his room, troubled. The locked door opens and LOUISE walks in.

LESTER: Look, I told you... Uh, I'm not receiving guests right now.

LOUISE: *(Entering.)* Un huh.

LESTER: What do you want?

LOUISE: Whatever you want.

LESTER: I want to be alone.

LOUISE: Me too. *(She stretches out on the bed exposing a naked thigh above her stockings.)*

LESTER: I have things to think about.

LOUISE: Are you always this boring?

LESTER: I don't...I don't expect you to understand. Please. There's the door.

LOUISE: Oh, I understand. You're in some sort of pain. That's why you're here.

LESTER: That's part of it.

LOUISE: Is the other half pleasure?

LESTER: Look...what do you want?

LOUISE: To see.

LESTER: See what?

LOUISE: If I want you or not. Do you love her?

LESTER: Who?

LOUISE: Your wife.

She turns on the TV. We hear moaning and music.

LESTER: I don't want to talk about my wife. *(He turns it off.)*

LOUISE: *(Whispering.)* That's it. Love isn't how close you get, it's how far you're willing to go.

She exits as PETER appears in his underwear.

Scene 8B

LESTER: What are you...? Get out of my room.!

PETER: I want everyone, you know. Everyone I see. Big asses, small asses, jiggle tits, flat chest. Even ugly girls. *(He pulls out a cigarette.)* I see lips pressed in pants like little open mouths longing for breath, you know, and I want them. Black, yellow, brown, blonde, brunette. It's not pretty. I know. But one isn't enough. Got a light?

LESTER: Where is she?

PETER: Who?

LESTER: My wife!

PETER: She's something else. Like playing accordion. What's the matter? Mano a mano. Is it a functionary thing?

LESTER: What?

PETER: You know, the hoist. What makes Pisa lean.

LESTER: Listen you idiot, where's my wife?

PETER: I don't know where she... Hold on...oh wait, wait...ya I think she's coming now.

Scene 8C

He disappears. There is a knock at the middle door LESTER answers; it's ARLENE dressed in a slip. She remains in the doorway

ARLENE: Lester, could you pick up some salmon steaks and croutons?

LESTER: Arlene, please Arlene.

ARLENE: I'll make you a nice supper.

LESTER: Arlene. Please don't do this.

ARLENE: But Lesto. This way you'll want me forever.

LESTER closes the door.

There is a knock at the S.R. door. LESTER opens it to see ARLENE and PETER kissing. She turns to LESTER.

ARLENE: I really do want the sofa re-upholstered.

They continue kissing. LESTER closes the door. There is a knock at the S. L. door. LESTER answers to see ARLENE and PETER having furious intercourse. ARLENE is bent forward and breathless.

Lester. *(Beat.)* You know *(Beat.)* I love you.

He closes the door.

The stage right door opens revealing the BELLHOP.

BELLHOP: Lester you know I love you.

The stage left door opens revealing PETER

PETER: Lester. You know I love you.

The middle door opens revealing ARLENE.

ARLENE: Salmon steaks and croutons.

LESTER closes one door after another. The knocking continues and increases. Then a symphony of knocking begins. It begins to take over LESTER's mind, he's reaching his wit's end as he falls to the floor and moans in misery. "Stop it. Stop it." He finally rises and runs to the middle door and opens it screaming…

LESTER: Go away!

It is ANTOINETTE the chambermaid. She is holding towels. They look at each other. Time freezes.

ANTOINETTE: Pardonnez-moi. *(She withdraws.)*

LESTER: No wait. Wait I'm…I'm…

               He looks down the hallway but she is gone.

Scene 9

               *He goes into his room. LESTER attempts to close
               the door but the BELLHOP appears as the Manager
               holding towels. He wears a suit and glasses.*

BELLHOP: Are you satisfied?

LESTER: What?

BELLHOP: Our policy is to ensure ultimate comfort. Are the
               accommodations satisfactory?

LESTER: Well the walls are a little thin and the floors creak.
               And the…

BELLHOP: When you've been around as long as this hotel,
               you'll make unpleasant noises too. I'd like to
               welcome you and bid you a fond repose. We think
               of our guests as ourselves. Your peace of mind is
               ours. Therefore the "Do Not Disturb" policy is
               strictly enforced enabling you to immerse yourself
               fully in the waters of reflection. *(Handing him the
               towels.)* These of course are to dry yourself.

LESTER: Is there a bar around here?

BELLHOP: Should you seek distraction during your stay.
               (Pulling out a Bible, hidden in the towels.) You may
               find it here.

LESTER: I'm not religious.

               The BELLHOP offers the book.

BELLHOP: To imbibe wisdom is not a religious pursuit.

               LESTER takes it.

You can expect your bed to be turned down regularly and a wake-up call whenever you decide. In any case, I am at hand should your spirit need refreshing.

LESTER: Thank you. That's very kind.

BELLHOP: It's my job. *(He exits.)*

Scene 10

LESTER crosses to the chair, sits and thinks. He is mentally exhausted. We hear crying through the walls. LESTER opens the bible and finds a flask inside. The sound of ticking begins to denote the passage of time. LESTER walks around the room. The ticking bleeds into footsteps that appear to be in the room. LESTER grows frightened. The room darkens. Tension builds. Finally LESTER's closet door bursts open and a figure dressed as LESTER at the top of the play in hat and trench coat holding a bouquet of flowers stands there. LESTER falls to the floor screaming and the door slams shut. The sounds cease. He is a wreck. He opens the flask and takes a healthy drink. He crosses cautiously and opens the closet. Only the hat and coat are hanging there. LESTER takes another drink.

Scene 11

The door opens. LOUISE appears and beckons LESTER to follow her. They cross through the hall and enter her room. They begin kissing. She throws her jacket on the floor and begins to pull off LESTER's. LESTER pulls out the flask and they drink. LOUISE leads him to the bed, pushes him down and gets on top of him grinding herself on him. She leans down to kiss him but licks his face instead, he tries to rise, she forces him back down. He tries again, she prevails, finally LESTER rolls her over aggressively and puts his hand up her dress. She begins to moan softly, it mounts until she finally comes. Her breathing is erratic. She struggles to catch her breath. She sits up and says:

LOUISE: Hand me my purse.

LESTER does and she pulls out an asthma respirator. She presses it twice. It is empty.

Ah shit.

Her heavy breathing continues. She pulls out a cigarette and lights it.

LESTER: Do you think that's a good idea?

She ignores him and continues smoking. Her breath is heavier.

What's the matter with your hands?

LOUISE: Eczema.

She smokes for a bit and continues gasping. Finally she puts out the cigarette.

I have to lie down.

She lies on the bed. LESTER is unsure what to do. He stands awkward, unsatisfied. She remains immobile, her breathing finally subsiding. LESTER tries to fit in behind her but cannot get comfortable. LOUISE stands up.

I need razor blades.

She leaves, closing the door and the light.

Scene 12

The fly buzzes. LESTER turns on the light. PETER is in bed smoking a cigarette. ARLENE enters wearing a dressing gown. PETER's in his underwear.

Randy Hughson and Veronika Hurnik.

ARLENE: Look…uh…Peter. It's time to go.

PETER: I might take a shower.

ARLENE: Lester will be home soon.

PETER: That's his name, Lester?

ARLENE: Come on, it's getting late.

PETER: He's not here?

ARLENE: He must have gone out.

PETER: Hunh. Were you thinking of him?

ARLENE: What?

PETER: When we were at it.

ARLENE: No.

PETER: You were saying something.

ARLENE: When?

PETER: In the pillow.

ARLENE: Don't burn the bed.

PETER: You were saying his name.

ARLENE: I wasn't.

PETER: What was it? What did you say?

ARLENE: Arlene.

        Pause.

PETER: Well that's fuckin' weird

ARLENE: I have to straighten up.

PETER: Will I see you again? Arlene.

ARLENE: Maybe… You should go.

PETER: But you haven't told me.

ARLENE: Told you what?

PETER: Why I'm here. What's the game.

ARLENE: It's nothing. Just a little fun.

PETER: Lester wasn't laughing.

ARLENE: You need money for a cab?

> *PETER laughs and kisses her neck.*

ARLENE: Please, I don't want him to see us.

PETER: Why not?

ARLENE: It's different after. It's a different thing.

PETER: You'd rather he caught us at it?

ARLENE: Never mind. Go.

> *Beat.*

PETER: Let me finish my smoke.

ARLENE: I have to change the bed.

PETER: Ya, Romeo's coming back. Pfft!

ARLENE: Let yourself out.

> *She starts to exit. He grabs her and pushes her onto the bed.*

PETER: What is it, Arlene? Do I disgust you now?

ARLENE: Don't be silly.

PETER: Have I soiled you?

ARLENE: Let me go!

PETER: I'm not gonna hurt you.

ARLENE: Please. My arm.

PETER: Tell me and I'll let you go.

ARLENE: No!

PETER: Tell me! Why won't Lester fuck you?

ARLENE: He stopped, all right! *(Beat.)* He just stopped! He lost interest or something. I don't know. Now let me go.

PETER: So you started shopping.

ARLENE: Please!

PETER: Bringing men home.

ARLENE: It's none of your fuckin'... Ah! Ah! Ah! He found me with someone...the first time in the living room.

PETER: And.

ARLENE: He watched us for half an hour. Then he made love to me every night for three weeks.

PETER: Why ?

            Pause.

ARLENE: He only wants me when I've been with someone else.

PETER: Is this a typical Friday evening?

ARLENE: It's happened a couple of times.

PETER: Hunh. But Lester didn't watch tonight.

ARLENE: No.

PETER: So something's changed. Maybe that's why he left.

            (He releases her.) There, I'm a man of my word. *(He begins to dress.)* You didn't ask me.

ARLENE: Ask you what?

PETER: Why I fucked you.

ARLENE: Please Peter. Just go.

PETER: You know, at the furniture store I thought she's kinda old but she's not a bag, you know. She prob'ly had a cocktail or two, looks like a bored, lonely woman. I thought I'd let you blow me. But when I saw Lester with that drowning face. Saying "Please don't do this." That's when I knew I'd bend you over.

ARLENE: Get off me!

PETER continues dressing.

ARLENE: Your shoes are under the bed.

PETER: Ya, thanks. *(He dresses in silence.)* It's been a pleasure, Arlene.

> *He kisses ARLENE on the forehead. She recoils and he exits. ARLENE sits for a bit as LESTER observes her. She is distressed. She rubs her arm and looks at the watch on her wrist. We hear the sound of a watch ticking and then stopping. She exits. LESTER sits on the bed alone.*

Scene 13

> *A telephone rings. LESTER, startled, cannot find the phone. Suddenly the BELLHOP appears from behind the headboard with a telephone.*

BELLHOP: Good evening. *(Pause.)* Oh, Mr. Monty... Yes of course.

> *As he takes the reservation, the BELLHOP sets up the lounge with chairs, liquor, and a bar extending the length of LESTER's bed.*

We're expecting you. Your reservation is secured.

(LESTER rings the bell.) I'll be right with you, Mr. Lester. *(Telephone)* Yes, a rest from the grind. I understand. I have a room I'm sure you'll find tranquil. *(Pause.)* Indeed, it's an elegant suite. The sheets are spun on the premises. *(To LESTER.)* He's a blabber. *(Telephone.)* Whenever, day or night, I'm always here.

LESTER:　　Is there a bar here?

BELLHOP:　*(Waving for LESTER to sit down.)* Quite private I assure you. *(Pause.)* We look forward to your stay. Hm?... Some company... Well Mr. Monty, I'll see what I can do.

> *He hangs up. A fly buzzes. The BELLHOP changes into the bartender. Location changes to the bar.*

Can't do anything about it. The place is a breeding ground. *(He hands LESTER a drink.)*

LESTER:　　I have them in my room too.

BELLHOP:　They're attracted to decaying matter. The maggots live off the residue in the bottles. Sometimes their eyes go red and they turn yellowy brown. *(Pause.)* Bar flies. You gonna stick around for the show?

Scene 14

> *Music plays. ESTELLE enters the bar talking to LOUISE. The BELLHOP provides them with beverages. They sit. ESTELLE has a book of dried flowers which she occasionally smells as she turns the pages. She speaks of a wonderful memory. LESTER eavesdrops as if it's his own past she speaks of.*

ESTELLE:　In the morning we'd make love, eat croissants with

almond filling, drink cafe au lait. Then we'd bathe and listen to Russian ballads as we washed and ate clementines he'd brought from Syria. Spitting seeds, pouring juice down our bodies. He'd pull himself from the bath and say "I will bake an angel cake." *(She giggles.)* Ooh Chrysanthemums. Smell these. *(She offers them to LOUISE, who declines.)* In the afternoon he fed me sliced bananas while I'd paint my toes and sing his favourite songs. Lilacs. I love lilacs.

She offers them to the bartender who exits to get a fresh bottle of bourbon.

We had a hammock stretched across the room that we'd lay in at night. Swinging and bouncing we'd read Pushkin, *The Rhyme of the Ancient Mariner, Il Purgatorio.* I'd wear his sailor hat while we made love and he'd whisper of the sea and how it called him. *(Suddenly sad.)* Then one day he left. *(Pause.)* But I do expect him shortly.

She closes her book. The lights change, the music shifts. We are in a fantasy.

ESTELLE turns and looks at LESTER.

ESTELLE: I walk down empty streets that whisper your name.

LOUISE: My eyes are red and running but there's no one left to blame.

ESTELLE: I think I'll dress in white tonight, my last remaining vice.

LOUISE: Or lay in bed like a book unread, in pages cold as ice.

The BELLHOP appears as a lounge singer. As he sings, the women begin to approach LESTER in the manner of spiders seeking prey. Crawling around him and biting his neck.

BELLHOP: She swings on a string
             Like a kite on a cloud
             But when it's time for dinner
             She's got eight legs all unbowed
             She's the red-and-white-legged widow.
             Some say she sleeps in silk
             Ooh some say she don't sleep at all
             But when she's crawling up my back
             I almost have a heart attack
             But if you dance
             You dance in fact
             With the red-and-white-legged widow.
             She's no Brown Recluse
             And she's no Tarantel
             But if she gets her fangs in you
             Your glands are gonna swell
             She's the red, I said
             You better check your bed, Lester!
             For the red-and-white-legged widow.

             *The lounge singer leaves. The women are in the
             same positions as before the fantasy. It has only
             occurred in LESTER's mind. The BELLHOP as
             bartender returns with a new bottle of bourbon.*

ESTELLE: *(To LESTER.)* I haven't seen you here before.

LESTER: I've been around.

ESTELLE: I'm sure you have. *(Intrigued.)* I don't believe I've
             had the pleasure.

LESTER: Lester.

ESTELLE: Estelle. Someone hurt you, Lester? Someone you
             loved? *(Silence.)* I've been hurt many times. Are
             you familiar with pain?

LESTER: I've had my share.

ESTELLE: When you've exceeded your share you'll know
             something about it. This is Louise. She's had her
             share.

The Bar. (l-r) Veronika Hurnik, Brenda Bazinet and Randy Hughson.

LESTER:	We've met.
ESTELLE:	*(She observes him intensely.)* There's something about you. I don't know what it is. Something about your mouth reminds me of… Why don't you come up for a nightcap? I'm in room one. *(She holds up her book.)* I'll show you my garden.
LESTER:	I'm not sure how long I'll be here.
ESTELLE:	Oh Lester. Do come. It's in full bloom.
LOUISE:	You can weed her beds.
LESTER:	No thank you.
ESTELLE:	Before it fades.
LESTER:	Maybe another time.
ESTELLE:	But I want to share it with you.
LESTER:	Look, I don't want to!
	He finishes his drink.
LOUISE:	You'll get drunk.
LESTER:	So I will.
LOUISE:	So will I. *(She touches LESTER's hand.)*
ESTELLE:	*(Hiding her hurt.)* If you'll excuse me. I have some peonies that need pressing. A pleasure, Mister Lester. I do hope you might reconsider. Straight to bed, Louise. Do attend to your condition. *(She exits.)*
LOUISE:	Goodbye.

Scene 14A

LESTER looks at LOUISE.

LESTER: That's your name, Louise? I'm Lester. *(Pause.)* Pleased to meet you.

LOUISE turns away and releases his hand.

LOUISE: I see through you like a piece of paper.

LESTER: So crumple me up and throw me away. *(Beat.)* I don't know about this place. I feel…out of my skin here. You ever feel out of your skin? I hear foot steps in my room and there's no one there.

LOUISE: I hear crying. Through the walls. A woman crying.

LESTER: What are you doing here?

LOUISE: My hands hurt, I'm going to bed. *(She stands.)*

LESTER: *(He stands.)* I'll walk you there.

Music changes LOUISE takes LESTER's hand and they begin to dance slowly as the BELLHOP begins to clean up the bar.

LOUISE: There's something about you. I don't know what it is.

LESTER: What?

LOUISE: You're a man's man, aren't you, Lester?

LESTER: What do you mean?

LOUISE: I don't know, I think maybe you're a man's man.

LESTER: You think I'm not a man?

LOUISE: Maybe it's not your wife at all.

LESTER: You've got me all wrong.

LOUISE: What do you want?

LESTER: I want to smell you, I want to touch your scars.

LOUISE: I can't let you see my badges. No no no no no.

LESTER: Come to my room.

LOUISE: How far are you willing to go?

LESTER: I don't know.

> *They exit. The bar is a bedroom again. The BELLHOP removes his shirt wearing a singlet beneath. He stretches out on the bed. He is now the Hustler.*

LESTER: *(Offstage.)* I don't think you had a purse.

> *LESTER returns to find LOUISE's purse. He sees the bar is gone and the BELLHOP on the bed. He turns to leave but the door closes. Another door opens and MONTY enters. LESTER scurries to the corner to watch in the shadows.*

Scene 15

> *MONTY is nervously holding a bottle of booze, checking the hallway for who might have seen him. He is out of breath. The BELLHOP is relaxed and looking for action. LESTER watches from the corner.*

MONTY: This hotel is creepy.

BELLHOP: I think it's pretty old.

> *They look at each other.*

MONTY: It's um...I think.

> *The BELLHOP touches MONTY. MONTY moves away.*

Uh, you want a drink? I have a bottle, um, I just need to get some ice.

He crosses to the door, the BELLHOP grabs his arm and pulls him close.

BELLHOP: I take it straight.

             Silence. They stare at each other.

MONTY: Um.

BELLHOP: What's your name.

MONTY: My name? Why do you want to know my name?

BELLHOP: So I could call you something.

MONTY: I go by Monty. You can call me Monty.

BELLHOP: Monty. That's a pretty name.

             Silence.

MONTY: I have a car here.

BELLHOP: I don't have anywhere to go.

             Sound of laughter.

MONTY: What was that?

BELLHOP: I didn't hear anything. Why don't we sit down. Monty.

MONTY: I...

BELLHOP: Just sit. There. That's not so bad is it?

MONTY: No. It's good. It's a firm bed. These old hotels have good beds. This is a good one.

BELLHOP: Yes it is. (*He takes MONTY's hand.*)

MONTY: My grandfather made beds. For a living.

BELLHOP: Oh yah. (*He places MONTY's hand on his crotch.*)

MONTY: Beautiful carved ones. He was a master. Finland.

BELLHOP: Finland.

MONTY: He was from Finland. I'm Finnish.

BELLHOP: Oh yah.

MONTY: A lot of craftsmanship to make a bed. *(He stands.)*
            Do you like this room? It's…I don't like this room.
            Listen, this was a bad idea. I'm sorry. I feel a little…
            I should go. This hotel is…I can't do this anymore.
            I have to go home. I'm married. I'm a married man.

BELLHOP: So what?

MONTY: You don't understand. You…you have sex with
            people for money. It's…it's different when you're
            married. You're only supposed to have sex with
            your partner. With your partner. The whole point
            of marriage is to prevent you from having sex with
            other people. Especially prostitutes. Especially
            men who are… Anyway I changed my mind. I
            have to go home. *(MONTY gathers his things.)*

BELLHOP: What if I was married?

MONTY: *(Stopping.)* Are you?

BELLHOP: Maybe.

MONTY: You're married? How could you be married?
            You're a prostitute and you're married? This is
            definitely a bad idea. How could you…does your
            wife know what you're doing? You're married and
            you're homosexual? You need help. I have to go.

BELLHOP: Monty. *(He approaches.)*

MONTY: Look I'll give you your money.

BELLHOP: Why did you change your mind?

MONTY: I uh, you're married. I can't.

BELLHOP: Because I'm married?

MONTY: Yes.

BELLHOP: If I were a single, bisexual prostitute you'd have no
            problem but if I'm married…

MONTY: You're bisexual? I definitely have to go. (*He breaks
            away.*)

BELLHOP: You're married.

MONTY: That's not the issue. The issue is your marriage.
            You're a gay married bisexual prostitute. You're
            the issue.

BELLHOP: Monty. Learn to fly. (*The BELLHOP begins to remove
            his pants and dance on the bed provocatively.*) Free
            yourself. Be who you want.

MONTY: Please leave the room. Please leave the room. I paid
            for the room. Look here's your money. I don't want
            you, please go, I'm the customer and I'm right…so
            go. (*He puts the money in the BELLHOP's underwear.*)
            Take the money. I don't want you. Take the money.

BELLHOP: You keep the money. (*He stuffs it in MONTY's
            mouth.*) You can buy a life full of happiness. How
            blissful your wife is shopping, while you enjoy a
            businessman's lunch. Have a nice stay.

            *He leaves. We hear the sound of jangling keys as he
            goes. MONTY shakes his head.*

MONTY: He needs help.

Scene 15A

            *LESTER crosses to exit the centre door. He opens it
            and sees that it is his room. He turns to MONTY.*

LESTER: Um, I think this is my room.

MONTY: What?

LESTER: I have key #3 and this is Room #3.

MONTY: What?

LOUISE appears with a purse.

LOUISE: Lester?

LESTER: Just a second. You're in the wrong room.

MONTY: Look I just came here for a rest, okay?

LESTER: This is my room.

LOUISE: Lester, my hands.

LESTER: Just a minute.

MONTY: Look buddy, this is the room they gave me.

LESTER: Listen!

MONTY: Hey I don't want any trouble.

LOUISE: Lester. I have to apply some ointment.

LESTER: Just a goddamn minute. I don't know how you got in here but...Louise. Where are you going...? Louise.

MONTY: Oh my, I have #5. I'm... This is...You shouldn't leave your door unlocked. Anyone could come in. *(He exits.)*

LESTER: Louise! Where did you go?

He closes the door. He is frustrated. ESTELLE enters through her door.

Scene 16

ESTELLE: I knew you'd come.

LESTER: What? This is... This is my room.

ESTELLE: How do I smell? Do I smell pretty?

LESTER: This is my…

ESTELLE: You never wrote. I thought of course you'd send a telegram.

LESTER: I don't know what you're talking about.

ESTELLE: Sing me some old song.

LESTER: Look, I'll show you. This is Room #3. *(He makes for door 3.)*

ESTELLE: *(Panicked.)* No don't go. You just arrived.

LESTER: Look lady…

ESTELLE: Did you bring me a memento?

LESTER: What?

ESTELLE: A gift. Quail eggs from Morocco or a mosaic from Shibam.

LESTER: No.

ESTELLE: *(Saddening.)* Some mountain essence from Constantinople?

LESTER: Lady I'm trying to tell you. I'm not who you think I am.

ESTELLE: But I've been waiting.

LESTER: I'm sorry, but it's not me. You'll have to wait somewhere else. Now get out. *(He tries to usher her out.)*

ESTELLE: I'm going. I said I'm going! No, you're not the man I thought you were. You're not the man at all.

            She exits.

Scene 17

We hear footsteps. ANTOINETTE slowly opens the door and looks around. LESTER is unseen behind it. She turns down the bed. LESTER peers from behind the door. The bed is ready. ANTOINETTE sees him.

LESTER: It's okay. I didn't mean to watch. I got caught behind the... Listen I wanted to say, about before...

Light change. Flash back.

ARLENE enters. LESTER focuses on her. She crosses to the bed. LESTER crosses to the bed and sits on the end. ARLENE begins kissing his neck. LESTER does not respond.

ARLENE: Are you tired?

LESTER: No it's just... I'm tense.

ARLENE: Oh.

LESTER: It's just work and everything.

ARLENE: Sure.

LESTER: I'll make it up to you.

ARLENE: Sure you will. *(Pause.)* Do you want to talk?

LESTER: No. It's nothing, I just feel. I just need a good night's sleep.

Pause.

ARLENE: Is it me?

LESTER: No. No no. Of course not, don't be stupid. It's me. I just need to relax.

Pause.

ARLENE: I'm going to get a book.

She exits.

LESTER: Wait. I wanted to say…

                (ANTOINETTE exits.) Wait. I wanted to say…

Scene 18

                The BELLHOP pops up dressed as a bartender and sets up the bar.

BELLHOP: It's always what you wanted to say, isn't it? That's the kicker. I seen this place filled with all kinds, and the thing of it is. There was always something left unsaid. *(He hands LESTER a bourbon.)*

LESTER: Have you seen the chambermaid?

BELLHOP: Chambermaid? I once saw a fellah crack a tumbler with his teeth and eat it. I watched a midget choke on a swizzle stick and cough it into a man's eye. I even seen a lady with a tongue like a pimento. But a chambermaid?

                MONTY stands at the entrance to the bar.

BELLHOP: You look like a martini man. *(MONTY enters.)* Some people you can tell their poison just by looking at their face. It stands out like the core of a boil. *(He pours the drink.)*

MONTY: Do you have any snacks?

BELLHOP: Reading faces is my business, knowing what the customer desires before he does. I see it before they even sit down.

MONTY: Peanuts? Crackers or something?

BELLHOP: My business is liquid.

MONTY: Ah, forget it.

LESTER: *(To MONTY.)* Have you seen the chambermaid?

MONTY:	What?
LESTER:	The chambermaid, I wanted to tell her... *(Recognizing MONTY.)* Did you find the right room?
MONTY:	What?
LESTER:	Remember? You were in my room.
MONTY:	What are you talking about? Are you trying to pick me up?
LESTER:	What? No. I thought you were in my room.
MONTY:	Listen buddy, you stay in your room, I'll stay in mine and everything will be fine. *(To BELLHOP.)* This guy hunh? Thinks I was in his room.

Pause.

LESTER:	So you haven't seen the chambermaid?
MONTY:	Listen I just came in for a...a...rest and now I'm having a drink. I'm not here with any...any woman. Okay. I don't know why you're pulling this stuff. I'm not looking for any acquaintance with anyone. *(To Bartender.)* Pickled eggs or anchovies?
LESTER:	Are you in pain?
MONTY:	Look buddy, I don't know what you're talking about.

Pause.

LESTER:	Are you married?
MONTY:	Will you stop?
LESTER:	Are you?
MONTY:	Yes I am very happily married, thank you very much. I don't need to explain it to anyone.

Alon Nashman, Randy Hughson and Richard Zeppieri.

LESTER:	Do you love her?
MONTY:	Oh Jesus. Who I love is none of your business.
LESTER:	How's your sex life?
MONTY:	How's my...? ...Listen guy, my sex life is none of your business. I don't even know why you're talking to me. You're probably a...a...bisexual prostitute or something.
	Silence.
MONTY:	Are you?
LESTER:	No. *(Pause.)* Do you only talk to prostitutes?
MONTY:	Listen pal, I've never talked to a prostitute in my life, God knows. I'm only passing through.
LESTER:	Un huh.
MONTY:	Not staying long.
LESTER:	No. *(Pause.)* I love my wife...
MONTY:	Good for you.
LESTER:	*(Struggling.)* Sometimes. Sometimes I... What about you? I've been trying to figure it out you know. And my wife. My wife sleeps with other men you see...sometimes. Sometimes she doesn't. It depends. But it's...did you say you loved your wife or not?
MONTY:	I'm a happily married man. I love my wife. I would never look at another woman and you sound very sick to me.
LESTER:	How could you not look at another woman?
MONTY:	Well that's the difference between you and me pal. I'm dedicated. I married for love. That counts for something.

BELLHOP:	Love is a web that connects you to everything.
MONTY:	You don't have to tell me. *(To LESTER.)* You could learn something from this guy.
LESTER:	I'm dedicated sometimes.

Enter LOUISE. LESTER stands.

Scene 19

LESTER:	Hello.

She sits and stares at MONTY. MONTY is uncomfortable.

LOUISE:	I haven't seen you here before.
MONTY:	I'm checking out very soon.
LOUISE:	You have an edge.
MONTY:	A what?
LOUISE:	Rugged jaw, piercing eyes. You're a man's man aren't you?
MONTY:	I'm just having a cocktail
LOUISE:	I'll bet you are. I'll join you.

The BELLHOP hands her a martini.

MONTY:	Look, I don't know what you want, but I'm really not interested. *(He stands up.)* I'm a happily married man okay. I'm not a...a man's man. I have no edge. I'm married. A happy man! Married. Okay?! *(He exits.)*
LESTER:	Do you think he's happy?
LOUISE:	Who cares.

Pause.

LESTER: I can't take this. I have to get out.

LOUISE: That's courageous.

LESTER: What do you say? This isn't the place for us. Let's take a trip. We'll get away from everything. Every lie. Every disappointment.

LOUISE: Where?

LESTER: Far away. Somewhere we've never been.

LOUISE: You and me?

LESTER: What do you say? Change ourselves.

LOUISE: No. I'll change. I like you as you are.

LESTER: Let's go now.

LOUISE: Can a girl finish her drink?

LESTER: The sooner the better.

LOUISE: I've been thinking about you. There's something about you that I like.

> *ARLENE, as a younger woman, enters and sits at the bar.*

LESTER: Before it's too late.

LOUISE: You're not like other men. I don't know what it is.

Scene 20

> *Flashback. Light change.*

LESTER: I don't know what it is.

ARLENE: I beg your pardon.

LESTER: No. I do. You'll think I'm stupid for saying this but... I've been observing you.

ARLENE: Oh.

LESTER: From over there. You're very beautiful.

ARLENE: I see.

LESTER: You're mysterious.

ARLENE: I suppose I'm flattered.

LESTER: Could you love me?

ARLENE: What? I don't even know your name.

LESTER: It's Lester.

ARLENE: Well Lester, my boyfriend might take exception to that.

LESTER: Is he here?

ARLENE: No.

LESTER: Then I'll take you home.

ARLENE: You'll do nothing of the kind.

LESTER: Do you love him?

ARLENE: My boyfriend? That's not very polite. I don't know.

LESTER: I could love you.

ARLENE: You've had too much to drink.

LESTER: No I haven't. I haven't. I don't usually say things like this. I'm not that kind of guy. I don't give my heart to anyone.

                They stare. ARLENE giggles shyly.

ARLENE: You're making me blush.

LESTER: What's your name?

ARLENE: I don't...

LESTER: You have a name don't you?

ARLENE: Arlene.

LESTER: Arlene, like a whisper. Arlene. You have long eye lashes Arlene.

ARLENE: No I don't.

LESTER: And emerald eyes.

ARLENE: No, I don't love him. *(Pause.)*

LESTER: Here, take my watch. Take it.

ARLENE: What for?

LESTER: As a gift.

ARLENE: I couldn't. It's too nice.

LESTER: As a present.

ARLENE: It stopped. It just stopped.

LESTER: Now it will always be the time we met.

            Beat.

ARLENE: Did you mean it, that you could love me?

LESTER: Yes.

ARLENE: And you'd never take it back?

LESTER: Never.

ARLENE: You're a very unusual man, Lester.

LESTER: Arlene.

            LESTER starts to toast her but LOUISE clinks his glass. End flashback. Lights return as before.

Scene 20A

LOUISE: You're a very unusual man, Lester. I don't know what it is. Wait. Yes I do. You're spineless. I find that attractive. I can shape you however I like. I can roll you into a ball and when I'm finished bouncing, just toss you away. *(She stands.)* I shaved my legs for you, Lesto.

> *ARLENE crosses to LESTER. They are both close to him. LESTER looks at one then the other. They address him.*

ARLENE: Are you going to walk away?

LOUISE: I'm already packed.

ARLENE: Is that what you want?

LOUISE: Lester. Let's go.

ARLENE: She'll never love you Lester.

BELLHOP: You can see it in their faces.

LOUISE: Not like me.

BELLHOP: Like the core of a boil.

LOUISE: Lester.

ARLENE: Lesto!

BELLHOP: The moment I saw you I saw bourbon.

ARLENE: Lester.

BELLHOP: Lester.

LESTER: What?

Scene 21

> *The women leave. The bartender hands LESTER a drink then continues to wipe a glass.*

BELLHOP: The rye smile. The corn mash eyes. You're a bourbon man.

LESTER: If you say so.

BELLHOP: I do. In fact, I see more bourbon in your face than I have in stock.

LESTER: Just fill it.

BELLHOP: *(He does.)* You must have a naughty secret, hunh? Some broken doll romance that eats you up .

LESTER: Mind your own business. *(He pops some pills.)*

BELLHOP: Who likes to do that? It's other people's business that's interesting.

LESTER: Let me drink in peace will ya.

> *The Figure dressed as LESTER in hat and coat, bent over, enters and sits at the bar. He carries a briefcase and a bouquet of flowers. We do not see his face.*

BELLHOP: Must be some pickle. *(Beat.)* Your wife?

LESTER: What about her?

BELLHOP: Whatsa matter? Not what you want?

LESTER: I married her, didn't I?

BELLHOP: Ya but you were a different person.

LESTER: Ahh.

BELLHOP: You were young. You bought into that whole thing. The myth of happiness. You're not the same man you were then.

LESTER: No.

BELLHOP: Then how can you be with the same woman?

            Beat.

BELLHOP: That luscious creature with the pout.

LESTER: What about her?

BELLHOP: She'd take away the pain. Who wouldn't want one of those in their stocking?

LESTER: It's not that simple.

BELLHOP: Everything is simple.

LESTER: No it isn't. I want it all.

BELLHOP: What's the matter with that? Put things in perspective. Once you stop wanting more, you dry up. Look at this guy, for example.

LESTER: Ya.

BELLHOP: Look how he sits. All slumped.

LESTER: What about it.

BELLHOP: Why d'ya think he sits like that?

LESTER: Maybe he has scoliosis. I don't know. What, do you want me to analyze this guy? Maybe he hates his job… Maybe his wife's cheating on him… Maybe he's on pills. Who knows? It's his problem.

BELLHOP: Classic. Wonders where the years went and what he's got to show.

LESTER: Shut up.

BELLHOP: Body's going. Feels unattractive.

LESTER: Hey just leave him alone.

BELLHOP: Trouble in the sack. Can't get it up.

LESTER: I said lay off.

BELLHOP: Maybe the wife calls out some other name in the
              dark.

LESTER: *(Grabbing him.)* Hey! Listen buddy...

BELLHOP: What if your wife was in someone else's arms right
              now? Whispering your name in someone else's
              mouth. Wouldn't it curve your spine?

LESTER: Don't, don't you...

BELLHOP: Mocking you with every thrust of her lover.
              Wouldn't it suck your guts?

LESTER: I can't...

BELLHOP: Wouldn't it gnaw your bones?

LESTER: I can't stop it!

BELLHOP: You don't deserve that.

LESTER: She's changed.

BELLHOP: What more can you say?

LESTER: It all comes down to sex with her.

BELLHOP: Classic.

LESTER: She got me doubting myself.

BELLHOP: No doubt.

LESTER: There's too much pressure.

BELLHOP: Do something for yourself.

LESTER: Start living again. Take what I want.

BELLHOP: Don't let love stop you .

LESTER: I don't need it. Screw the world! The whole stupid
              planet! I'm gonna do things for myself from now

on. I'll watch what I want. Eat what I please. Drink till I'm sick. Go to bed with whom I choose. And take something for myself. I don't need anybody!

Pause. The figure in the hat and coat exits.

BELLHOP: Can I get you another?

LESTER: No, I think I've had enough. Where'd that guy go?

BELLHOP: What guy?

LESTER: There was a guy sitting there a second ago.

BELLHOP: I don't know what you're talking about, mister.

The bar is transformed into LESTER's room again. The BELLHOP fluffs his pillows. LESTER lays down to rest.

BELLHOP: Goodnight.

The BELLHOP exits.

Scene 22

The Nightmare

LESTER lies on the bed. We hear distant sounds in the hotel. LESTER is uneasy. One by one the five doors around him begin to open part way. Close and open. They call his name in different creaking tones. LESTER is awake and panicked. He hears the following echoing, distorted dialogue in a growing wash of sound [Recorded sound in italics].

PETER: Is it a functionary thing?

ARLENE: He just stopped!

MONTY: My sex life is none of your business.

ARLENE: He only wants me when I've been with someone else.

ARLENE:	*Uh hunh, unh, unh. Unh!*
BELLHOP:	Trouble in the sack. Can't get it up.
ARLENE:	He lost interest or something.
BELLHOP:	Wouldn't it curve your spine?
ARLENE:	*Yes. Yes. Yes.*
ARLENE:	*Do you want to talk about it?*
MONTY:	The issue is your marriage.
ARLENE:	Is it me?
ESTELLE:	They're private. My private things.
ARLENE:	*He watched us for half an hour.*
ARLENE:	*Oh ya, ya, ya.*
ESTELLE:	Are you familiar with pain?
BELLHOP:	You must have a naughty secret, hmm?
ARLENE:	Is it me?
MONTY:	You sound very sick to me.

LESTER bolts up in bed, overwhelmed by his mind.

LOUISE:	You're spineless. I find that attractive.
ARLENE:	Is it me?
LOUISE:	How far are you willing to go?
ARLENE:	Lester, you know I love you.

> *LESTER is at the edge. The sound is building to a crescendo. We hear the immense sound of something cracking open—LESTER's mind or heart. LESTER screams.*

The Nightmare. Randy Hughson.

Scene 23

> *ANTOINETTE enters, turns on the light and sees
> LESTER. He is clearly unhinged.*

ANTOINETTE: Monsieur. *(Beat.)* Pardon.

LESTER: Don't go.

ANTOINETTE: Je ne comprend pas.

LESTER: Please. Please. I just wanted to...I just wanted to
            say...I'm sorry. I'm sorry. I'm so sorry. *(He begins to
            weep uncontrollably.)* Help me. I don't. I don't know
            what to do anymore. I don't know what to...I love
            her but...I can't feel anything. All those years
            and... I look at her and... I feel nothing. I
            just...want to be happy. I just want to... It's me, I
            know it's my fault. I know. But what can I do? I
            want...I want to start again...

> *He is empty. ANTOINETTE moves to him and
> touches his hand.*

ANTOINETTE: Monsieur. La vie n'est pas si dur que ca. La vie,
            c'est une fleur qu'on arose par coeur. *(She touches
            his heart.)* Et la; il ya un fleuve.

> *(Mister. Life isn't as hard as that. Life is a flower that
> you water. From your heart. There's a river there.)*

> *ANTOINETTE goes to the closet and gets his hat,
> coat and briefcase. She puts them down and moves
> to exit. She opens the door to leave and all the doors
> open, flooding the room in white light. LESTER is
> on his knees, transformed.*

Scene 24

> *Music plays. LESTER dresses in his hat and coat.*
> *He picks up the bouquet of flowers now withered*
> *and dead. He places them on a pillow with his room*
> *key. ESTELLE enters her door looking at her flower*
> *book. LOUISE enters her door rubbing ointment*
> *into her hands. MONTY enters his door pouring a*
> *drink. They arrive and depart like ghosts LESTER*
> *is imagining. LESTER leaves his room and walks*
> *down the hall as the BELLHOP emerges from*
> *behind the headboard.*

Scene 25

BELLHOP: And in its quest for freedom the fly employs every
            ounce of strength to break the silver bonds that
            hold him in his place. As the black beast tiptoes
            towards him, over steely strands that know no
            bend. But once, I saw a fly break free from the
            hands of disaster. As the tiny thing struggled at its
            impending doom, beneath its feet the web gave
            way, and the fly flew from its prison to live another
            day. Without a memory of what went before. Its
            existence was all it knew.

> *The hotel transforms back into LESTER and*
> *ARLENE's house at the beginning of the play. The*
> *BELLHOP exits as ARLENE enters and takes the*
> *same position as at the top of the play.*

Scene 26

We hear keys jangle and the door opens. LESTER enters holding a bag of groceries. The tableau is reminiscent of his entrance at the top of the play. ARLENE looks at him and then turns away.

Black out.

The End

What the Critics are saying about *This Hotel*

"Sharp, snazzy and sexy. A journey into the mysterious corridors and rooms that fill the mind of the cuckolded and indecisive Lester, *This Hotel* is a psychological spree of sadness and seduction."
—*NOW Magazine*

"Sizzles with theatrical charge...crammed with fascinating material."
—*Back Stage*

"Sharp, funny and often touching. *This Hotel* is well on its way to being an important Canadian play."
—*Eye Magazine*

"Delicious mind-bending stuff that creates a certain order out of the contained chaos of Poch-Goldin's delightfully demented and sexy script."
—*Toronto Sun*

"Absurdly hilarious and deliciously sexy, Alex Poch-Goldin's new work signals what may very well be a renaissance in Canadian theatre."
—*Toronto On Stage*